Next Generation
ENERGY

ENERGY FROM LIVING THINGS

Biomass Energy

Rachel Stuckey

CRABTREE
Publishing Company
www.crabtreebooks.com

Crabtree Publishing Company

www.crabtreebooks.com

Author: Rachel Stuckey

Editors: Sarah Eason, Jen Sanderson, and Shirley Duke

Proofreader: Katie Dicker and Wendy Scavuzzo

Editorial director: Kathy Middleton

Design: Paul Myerscough and Geoff Ward

Cover design: Paul Myerscough

Photo research: Sarah Eason and Jen Sanderson

Prepress technician: Margaret Amy Salter

Print coordinator: Margaret Amy Salter

Consultant: Richard Spilsbury, degree in Zoology, 30 years as an author and editor of educational science books

Written and produced for Crabtree Publishing by Calcium Creative

Photo Credits:

t=Top, bl=Bottom Left, br=Bottom Right

Dreamstime: Bertold Werkmann: p. 16; Gnomeandi: p. 15; Igor Bar: p. 4; Ken Wolter: p. 18; Photographerlondon: p. 21; Photomailbox: pp. 18–19; PN Photo: p. 17; Sam Chadwick: p. 8; Scanrail: p. 20; Tan Kian Yong: p. 26; Xicoputini: pp. 14–15; NASA: Reto Stöckli/Nazmi El Saleous/Marit Jentoft-Nilsen/NASA GSFC: pp. 4–5; Shutterstock: AFNR: p. 19; Alberto Masnovo: p. 1; Curraheeshutter: p. 27; Djgis: p. 6; Dudarev Mikhail: pp. 16–17, 32; Fluke Samed: pp. 6–7; FotoBug11 pp. 3, 20–21; Fotohunter p. 9; Frontpage: p. 22; Konstantin Romanov: pp. 22–23; KPG Payless: pp. 3, 12; Lukas Pobuda: p. 7; Marcel Clemens: pp. 8–9; Marco Prati: p. 14; Nataliya Hora: p. 10; Oskari Porkka: p. 24; PanicAttack: pp. 24–25; Pavel Hlystov pp. 12–13, 28–29; PhotographyByMK: pp. 10–11, 30–31; Racorn: p. 23; RGtimeline: p. 11; Rob Marmion: p. 28; Stephane Bidouze: pp. 26–27; Wikimedia Commons: Gary Tarleton/Library of Congress and Prints, Washington: p. 13; U.S. Navy/Kelly Schindler: p. 25.

Cover: Shutterstock: Alberto Masnovo.

Library and Archives Canada Cataloguing in Publication

Stuckey, Rachel, author
    Energy from living things : biomass energy / Rachel Stuckey.

(Next generation energy)
Includes index.
Issued in print and electronic formats.
ISBN 978-0-7787-1980-9 (bound).--
ISBN 978-0-7787-2003-4 (paperback).--
ISBN 978-1-4271-1638-3 (pdf).--ISBN 978-1-4271-1630-7 (html)

    1. Biomass energy--Juvenile literature. I. Title.

TP339.S79 2015   j333.95'39   C2015-903214-8
                                      C2015-903215-6

Library of Congress Cataloging-in-Publication Data

Stuckey, Rachel, author.
  Energy from living things : biomass energy / Rachel Stuckey.
    pages cm. -- (Next generation energy)
  Includes index.
  ISBN 978-0-7787-1980-9 (reinforced library binding : alk. paper) --
ISBN 978-0-7787-2003-4 (pbk. : alk. paper) --
ISBN 978-1-4271-1638-3 (electronic pdf : alk. paper) --
ISBN 978-1-4271-1630-7 (electronic html : alk. paper)
1. Biomass energy--Juvenile literature. 2. Renewable energy sources--Juvenile literature. 3. Agriculture and energy--Juvenile literature. I. Title.

TP339.S787 2016
333.95'39--dc23

                    2015022001

Crabtree Publishing Company

www.crabtreebooks.com   1-800-387-7650

Printed in Canada/082015/BF20150630

Published in Canada
Crabtree Publishing
616 Welland Ave.
St. Catharines, Ontario
L2M 5V6

Published in the United States
Crabtree Publishing
PMB 59051
350 Fifth Avenue, 59th Floor
New York, New York 10118

Published in the United Kingdom
Crabtree Publishing
Maritime House
Basin Road North, Hove
BN41 1WR

Published in Australia
Crabtree Publishing
3 Charles Street
Coburg North
VIC, 3058

Contents

What Is Biomass?

Biomass comes from plants and other organic matter such as animal and human waste. Biomass is renewable because it is part of the life cycle of our planet. There is a limited amount of energy in the universe—new energy cannot be created, we can only reuse the energy that already exists. When biomass is used to generate power, the by-products are eventually used to create more biomass by returning carbon to the soil. This is called the carbon cycle.

Plants use water, **carbon dioxide**, and energy from the Sun to grow through the process of **photosynthesis**. People use the energy stored in plants in many ways. They eat them to give their bodies energy. The energy in plants is also used to generate heat, light, and power. If you have ever made a campfire, you have used biomass.

Biomass is part of our planet's life cycle. Using biomass is one way to create renewable, **sustainable** energy.

A Renewable Energy

Only about 11 percent of energy in the United States is renewable, and biomass makes up about half of that. Canada uses more hydroelectric power, which is electricity created from moving water. There biomass is the second most common source of renewable energy.

Other countries around the world use much more biomass energy. Finland and Sweden use biomass for large portions of their heat and electricity. Some people in Germany and Austria heat their homes using wood pellets created from sawdust and other waste from lumber. Many parts of the developing world rely on biomass for cooking and heating. Biomass can include trees and **crops**, which are plants grown for food. It can also come from waste such as used cooking oil, leftover pieces of lumber, or even cow dung or manure.

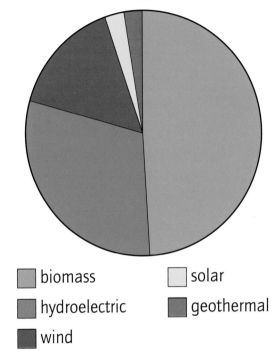

Renewable Energy Use in the U.S.

- biomass
- hydroelectric
- wind
- solar
- geothermal

Biomass energy is the most common form of renewable energy used in the United States.

The Energy Future: You Choose

There is a myth that says more electricity, heat, and fuel is needed to grow, harvest, and convert biomass into energy than the energy generated by that biomass. However, this is not true. Corn **ethanol** produces 50 percent more energy, and it requires less energy than most other types of biomass. However, biomass does have less energy per pound than **fossil fuels**, so it takes more energy to transport it. What can we do to make sure biomass is an efficient source of energy? Is it possible for technology in the future to play a part in moving and using biomass?

The History of Biomass

Biomass is the oldest source of power. When humans first learned to make fire, they were using biomass. For hundreds of thousands of years, biomass was the only way humans could cook their food and generate heat and light. Today, many parts of the developing world rely on biomass for fuel in their homes. Wood, animal dung, and other organic materials are used for cooking food and heating homes.

While biomass may be old, its name is very new. In the 1970s, the use of fossil fuels such as oil became very expensive. People also started to worry about the **pollution** created by fossil fuels and that these fuels may some day run out. Scientists started to look for more reliable and inexpensive sources of energy. Soon, the idea of using organic material on a large scale caught on, and scientists started using terms such as "bioenergy," "biofuel," and "**biomass**." Biomass refers to the solid material used to create fuels, and eventually, energy.

Animals can be a source of biomass energy. This cow's manure can be used to generate electricity on farms.

Biomass Today

At first, researchers thought biomass would quickly become popular. However, the development of biomass technology has happened slowly. Today in North America, the most commonly used biomass is ethanol created from corn. Most gasoline contains some ethanol. There are also some power plants that burn different types of biomass, along with coal, to generate electricity. Some communities have power plants that burn waste to create electricity. The use of biomass is growing in the race to reduce the use of fossil fuels.

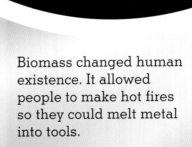

Biomass changed human existence. It allowed people to make hot fires so they could melt metal into tools.

REWIND

One of the most important developments in human history was learning how to use biomass to make and control fire. Evidence suggests that some humans were using fire more than 1 million years ago. With fire, humans could cook their food and create warmth and light. They could also cook and store extra food. This gave them time to do other things, such as create art and learn to communicate with each other. People also started sharing food and building communities. What other ways do you think fire and biomass helped build human **civilization**? Explain your thinking. How did the discovery of fire lead to the use of early technology?

Renewable Biomass

Being part of the carbon cycle is what makes biomass a renewable energy source. Solar power and wind power are also renewable sources of energy. The advantage of biomass is that it can be stored and used when needed —it does not depend on sunny or windy days.

Oil and coal come from ancient biomass. They were created from the remains of plants and animals that died millions of years ago, which is why they are called fossil fuels. They take so long to be created that the oil and coal that exist on Earth today cannot be replaced. When we use this source of energy, it is gone forever—it is nonrenewable. When we burn these fuels, we change them into carbon dioxide and other gases that are harmful to the **atmosphere**.

Many power plants in North America generate electricity by burning coal. Coal is a fossil fuel, and fossil fuels are nonrenewable.

The Carbon Cycle

All living things are made of carbon. Burning biomass or fuels created from biomass gives off carbon dioxide. This carbon dioxide, however, is part of the carbon cycle. Plants use the Sun's energy to create carbon from water and carbon dioxide through photosynthesis.

Some plants are used as food—animals, including humans, can get the energy they need by eating the plants so their bodies can use the carbon they contain. The carbon in plants is also used to generate heat, light, and power. When plants are converted into energy, carbon dioxide gas is released into the air. In the carbon cycle, other plants use this carbon dioxide to create carbon through photosynthesis again.

Plants grow by converting the Sun's energy. People use the energy stored in plants to fuel themselves and their world.

FAST FORWARD

When fossil fuels are burned, carbon dioxide is given off, creating too much carbon dioxide for today's carbon cycle. Instead, the gas creates the **greenhouse effect**, which has lead to **climate change**. What if the carbon cycle cannot recycle the carbon dioxide generated from biomass energy? Throughout history, people have chopped down trees for energy, to build things, to create farmland, and to build cities. If they continue to clear the forests, they will destroy Earth's ability to continue the carbon cycle. For biomass to be a renewable energy source, trees and other plants need to be protected. What can you do to help maintain the carbon cycle? Why is it important?

Getting to the Power

Any organic material can be used as biomass, but some materials are better than others. All biomass begins as a solid such as wood, or a liquid such as cooking oil, which is extracted or taken out of solids.

Solid biomass can be used to generate **thermal**, or heat, energy, just like in a cooking fire. It can also be used in power plants, and the heat it creates can be used to warm people's homes. The heat can also be used to generate electricity using steam **turbines**. This is called **thermal conversion**, which is changing any biomass using heat into forms of energy.

Solids can also be converted into gas and liquid form using **chemical conversion** and **biochemical conversion**. **Gasification** is a chemical conversion process that turns solids into gases. In biochemical conversions, bacteria and other **microorganisms** feed on organic matter. The waste created by the organisms can be used as a fuel. When organic matter rots, it produces methane gas, which can be burned as a fuel. Another biochemical process called **fermentation**, can turn the sugars in corn and other plant materials into ethanol.

Microorganisms, such as bacteria, yeast, and mold, break down biomass by eating it. The organisms' waste products can be used as fuel.

The Next Generation

When crops are grown specifically for generating energy, they are called first generation biomass. This means their first use was for power. Second generation biomass fuels come from waste—when the second use of the plants is for power. Second generation fuels are harder to make. For the same reason that people cannot eat corn stalks and husks, making efficient fuel from this type of biomass material is harder to do. However, scientists are working to find new ways to make second generation biomass energy.

Corn is a source of first generation biomass energy. In North America, it is grown to make ethanol fuel.

FAST FORWARD

The town of Reynolds, Indiana, may be the most energy-efficient town in the United States. A special project called BioTown USA began in 2006. The energy used in Reynolds comes from local alternative sources. The town's vehicles run on fuels made from biomass. The town converts animal waste into electricity and natural gas, and it uses what is left to **fertilize** crops. The goal of the project is to make farming sustainable and self-sufficient by generating its own power. If the project is successful, how do you think it could be used to help change the way people live elsewhere?

The Solid State of Biomass

Biomass begins as a solid, but burning solids creates a lot of air pollution. Throughout history, many things have been done to protect against this pollution and make solid biomass more efficient.

One of the first changes was switching from wood to charcoal. Charcoal is made by burning wood slowly in a closed space with very little oxygen. For thousands of years, humans around the world have used charcoal because it burns longer and hotter than regular wood. When charcoal is made, the impurities in the wood are burned away. This made charcoal fires cleaner than wood fires when used in homes and workplaces, making it better for those breathing the air around the fire.

Charcoal generates a fire that is hotter than a wood fire.

REWIND

Hundreds of years ago, Europe began using wood faster than new trees could grow. Soon, Europeans started replacing charcoal with coal that was mined from the ground and coal became the main source of power. Coal fires burned hotter than charcoal and also produced less soot and smoke. However, burning coal released many hidden pollutants, such as sulfur and greenhouse gases. Mining coal is also a dangerous job. Coal was used to power ships, trains, factories, and even homes, during the **Industrial Revolution** and in the 1800s, it was used to generate electricity. Why do you think biomass fuel might seem to be such an attractive alternative when people consider the effects of burning traditional fuels such as coal? What would be the differences in the effects of coal as fuel compared to biomass as fuel?

Bringing Biomass Back

There is a large supply of coal in North America. Today, coal is the most common source of electricity in the United States and the third most common in Canada. Mining coal is very bad for the environment and is a dangerous job. In some places, biomass is coming to the rescue. One way to reduce the environmental costs of coal is to **co-fire** coal with biomass. To co-fire is to burn two different materials together. Co-firing creates the same amount of electricity, but uses less coal. Using less coal reduces air pollutants. Co-firing also allows communities to use biomass without having to build biomass power plants.

The Hull-Oakes Sawmill is the last steam-powered lumber mill in the United States. Waste from cutting the lumber is used to power the mill.

Waste Not, Want Not

Although burning biomass produces air pollution, one of the best things about biomass energy is that it can be created from waste products, which can reduce pollution in other ways.

After crops are harvested, the part of the plants that cannot be eaten can be used as second generation biomass. The leaves, weeds, and trimmed branches from parks and backyards can also be used as second generation biomass. Another way is to use household garbage to create energy. When animals and humans eat plants and other animals, their own waste products can even be used as second generation biomass.

Animal Dung

Humans have been using animal waste for fueling fires almost as long as they have used wood and charcoal. Dried animal dung, or waste, can be collected and stored, then used in a fire. Animal dung is often used in regions with few trees. When American pioneers crossed the Great Plains, they used the dung of wild buffalo, known as buffalo chips, to build fires. In parts of India today, many people collect dung from cows and water buffalos to fuel fires.

Pioneers on the Great Plains collected buffalo chips to use as fuel.

Indoor Air Pollution

Using animal dung to generate energy is a great example of second generation biomass energy. Also, collecting animal dung for use in fires prevents it from polluting the ground and water. However, burning animal dung pollutes the air. About 3 billion people around the world must burn solid fuels, such as wood or animal dung, to heat their homes and cook their food. This creates very dangerous air pollution in their homes. The particles from household fires get deep into their lungs and can cause many health problems.

An Indian woman carries a basin full of cow dung on her head. The dung will be caked, dried, and used as cooking fuel for the people in her village.

FAST FORWARD

Many people have no access to clean water because their water sources are polluted with **sewage**. The Omni Processor is a new technology that can separate the solids from the water in sewage. The processor then uses the solid materials to power a water treatment system. Not only is clean drinking water produced from the sewage, but the biomass in the sewage also generates extra electricity. The inventors call it a self-sustaining bioenergy process. How do you think the development of this technology could change the way people in developing countries live?

Lighter Than Air

Gases are a form of matter that have air-like qualities and spread out through the air. Some gases are flammable, so they burn easily, which makes them good fuels. Gases burn more efficiently than solids. Gasification is a process that converts solid material into gas by heating it to more than 1,292° Fahrenheit (700° C) without burning. This process is often used to generate power from coal.

When gasification is used with biomass, it creates a renewable energy source called biogas. The biogas produced through gasification can be used the same ways as any other gas—to heat homes, cook food, and even power vehicles.

Another way to generate biogas is through **anaerobic** digestion. Anaerobic means without using oxygen. The microorganisms eat the biomass and produce a combination of gases and other waste products, which can be burned. The solid that is left can be used as a fertilizer. This method of creating biogas has been used for centuries all around the world. The most common use today is on farms.

In large plants such as this, biomass is converted into gas that can be piped through gas lines to homes and businesses.

On the Farm

Farms around the world are using biodigesters to generate their own energy. Anaerobic digestion turns manure and agricultural waste into heat and electrical power. Biodigestion also reduces the **odor**, or smell, of the manure. Farms with a lot of animals, such as dairy farms, can produce more electricity than the farm needs. These farmers can sell the extra power to the local **power grid**. By using this second generation biomass to create their electricity, farms can be self-sustaining, saving money and the environment!

When garbage is covered over in landfills, it starts to break down and produce methane gas. Methane gas can be turned into heat and electricity.

The Energy Future: You Choose

A landfill is a large garbage dump where waste is buried or covered over with earth and other materials. When the waste breaks down, methane gas is created. This gas must be released into the atmosphere so the landfill does not catch fire or explode. Instead of releasing the gas, some companies collect it for use as a fuel. Some scientists say this is not renewable energy because it is created from waste. Activists want people to reduce, reuse, and recycle so that they do not need landfills. Do you think more landfill gas power plants should be built? Find examples in this book to support your answer.

Fermenting for Fuel

Biomass can be used to create liquid fuels to use in vehicles. One of the most common biomass fuels is ethanol. Ethanol is a popular alternative to fuels such as gasoline and diesel, which are made from crude oil. Ethanol is blended with gasoline in the United States and Canada.

Ethanol is made through the process of fermentation, which is a type of biochemical conversion. Humans have been using yeast since ancient times to make bread and drinks such as beer. Yeast is a microorganism that feeds on sugar. The yeast organisms create carbon dioxide gas that makes bread rise and forms an alcohol called ethanol.

Not only can ethanol be used in place of fossil fuels, but it also creates less air pollution than regular gasoline. Most ethanol is made from crops that are grown specifically for making ethanol. However, ethanol can also be made from agricultural waste. This is called cellulosic ethanol because it is made from cellulose—the parts of plants that cannot be eaten.

By fermenting corn with yeast organisms, this refinery in the Midwest creates ethanol fuel.

Brazil and Sugar Cane

In the United States, most ethanol is made from corn. Other parts of the world make ethanol from corn, sugar cane, or other high **carbohydrate** crops. Brazil is the world's largest grower of sugar cane and the global leader in biofuel. Brazil started making ethanol from sugar cane in the 1920s for use in cars. In the 1970s, Brazil changed the laws so that all gasoline sold in the country had to be blended with ethanol. Today, cars sold in Brazil have flexible fuel engines that can run on gasoline, blended gasoline, or pure ethanol.

This ethanol plant in São Paulo, Brazil, makes fuel from sugar cane. Brazil is a world supplier of sugar cane.

REWIND

The very first cars had engines that ran on biofuels or fuels made from biomass. In 1890, Rudolf Diesel built an engine that ran on plant oils. Today, that engine is known as a diesel engine and its fuel is usually made from oil. Further back, in 1826, Samuel Morey invented an engine that ran on ethanol, which was a very common fuel for lamps and stoves. As a result of a special tax, ethanol became more expensive, so gasoline engines became more popular. How could tax be used to change our fuel choices today? Explain your thinking. What would be the long-term effect on global climate change?

Fill 'er Up!

Most cars in North America today run on gasoline, but trucks use diesel. Diesel engines work differently from gasoline engines. They are also more powerful and more fuel-efficient. Most diesel fuel comes from crude oil today, but when Rudolf Diesel first invented his engine, he ran it on peanut oil.

Diesel cars are not as popular in North America, because for a long time the engines were loud and had dirty exhausts. However, diesel engines have improved over time, and are now much cleaner and quieter. Just like the original, today's diesel engines can also run on **biodiesel**, which is diesel fuel made from vegetable or animal biomass instead of crude oil.

While ethanol is made from the sugars in biomass, biodiesel is made from the fat or oil. The fats are extracted from plants or animals, and mixed with alcohol to produce **methyl esters** and **glycerin**. Methyl esters are the biodiesel and glycerin is a useful by-product used to make other things such as soap. Some common sources of biodiesel are palm oil, canola oil, soybean oil, and fish oil.

Like gasoline, biofuel can be transported across the country on train cars.

The Biodiesel Market

All the buses in Halifax, Nova Scotia, ran on biodiesel for several years. In 2004, the city started using a fuel made from 80 percent regular diesel and 20 percent fish oil diesel. Unfortunately, biodiesel is still a new idea and right now it costs more than regular diesel. The company that made the fuel for Halifax's buses had to stop production because they did not have enough customers.

Most biodiesel is sold in blends with normal diesel. It is possible to run a regular diesel car on blended or pure biodiesel, but most carmakers do not recommend it. However, Chevrolet introduced a new car in 2014 that is designed to run on 20 percent biodiesel blend.

Diesel engines can be modified to run on regular plant-based cooking oil.

FAST FORWARD

With modifications, diesel engines can also run on pure cooking oil. Some people collect waste deep-fryer oil from local restaurants to power their cars. Now McDonald's has joined the club. In some countries, McDonald's uses its waste French fry oil to power its own delivery trucks. This effort prevents waste and pollution, and replaces the use of fossil fuels. Cooking oil is expensive, so it makes sense to recycle it. However, engines must be converted to run on pure cooking oils. Do you think used cooking oil might replace gasoline more widely in the future? How might that work in practice? What problems must be solved to use it on a widespread scale?

What Is Wrong with Biomass?

Biomass does have some problems. Building new power plants is very expensive. Producing electricity from biomass is only efficient where there is a source nearby—transporting biomass long distances is not worth the cost. This makes it unlikely that biomass could supply energy for large areas in the way the current power grid does. Biomass is also seasonal, because only tropical countries can grow and harvest biomass year-round.

A lot of land is needed to grow biomass, even if it comes from waste. Using ethanol works for Brazil because the country has the land needed to grow sugar cane. If the United States wanted to use 100 percent corn ethanol instead of gasoline, it would need to grow corn in an area the size of the continental United States!

To make enough land to grow energy crops, rain forests are being cut down. That action is a threat to the carbon cycle.

Sustainable or Not?

Biomass also causes environmental problems. Scientists now believe that the carbon cycle does not absorb as much carbon dioxide from biomass energy as they first thought. Also, using waste material for energy can release harmful substances into the air. We also know that many people burn biomass in open fires, which creates a large amount of household air pollution. Using biomass in large amounts, such as making fuel from corn, encourages overproduction. Growing large amounts of corn may not be the best use of land. If more land is needed for growing energy crops, it may lead to chopping down more and more forests. If produced in this way, biomass power is not sustainable, which is the goal of renewable energy.

Using good farmland to grow energy crops could cause the possibility of food shortages around the world.

The Energy Future: You Choose

Supporters say that energy crops are a great renewable energy source. But others argue that good farmland should be used to grow food. Also, growing large amounts of the same crop year after year ruins the soil. Good farming practice rotates, or changes, crops every few years. Critics also worry that if wealthy countries pay poorer tropical countries to grow energy crops, poor countries will chop down important rain forests and use up all their land. This will damage the environment and prevent poor countries from being able to grow their own food, which will lead to possible food shortages.
Are energy crops a good idea? Give examples from this book and other resources to support your answers.

Benefits of Biomass

No source of energy is perfect—yet. Even though biomass has some problems, it also has great potential. If resources are well managed, biomass is renewable. With creative thinking and careful use, biomass can help us build a more sustainable environment.

Biomass may not be able to produce large amounts of power all over North America, but it can provide power at a local level. This would give communities control over their energy needs. Communities with good sources of biomass can make use of the technology. Individual farms can create their own electricity so they do not have to depend on other sources. Parts of the world with good, sustainable energy crops can take advantage of biomass energy to their own benefit. As researchers continue to experiment with biomass, they learn more efficient ways to develop second generation biomass energy that will work for some communities.

Scientists continue to look for ways to use biomass to generate renewable energy.

The Green Hornet runs on a blend of half jet fuel and half biofuel made from the camelina plant.

Harnessing Waste

Many communities are using waste-to-energy systems to deal with their solid waste problem and to generate energy. The Isle of Wight in the United Kingdom has a power plant that uses the island's garbage to generate electricity. The plant dries the garbage and uses gasification to create a gas that is burned to generate electricity. Before this plant opened, the island had to transport waste out for disposal on the mainland of England. The ash from burning the waste is also used on the island's landfill. From dealing with industrial waste, household trash, used cooking oil, and even sewage, biomass energy systems can help solve two problems at once.

The Energy Future: You Choose

The Environmental Protection Agency (EPA) reports that people in the United States create 260 million tons (236 million tonnes) of garbage every year! Recycling and composting can help reduce waste. Using municipal solid waste (MSW) as a source of biomass could help solve the waste problem. However, the Union of Concerned Scientists warns that waste-to-energy plants create high levels of air pollution. Waste-to-energy is not really renewable energy because it may encourage people to consume more and create more waste. Do you think building waste-to-energy plants is a good solution? Explain your thinking. How has technology changed the way we view garbage?

Biomass of the Future

Biomass today has many limitations and poses some risks. However, researchers are always working on the problem. The Omni Processor may someday bring clean water to communities in developing countries. Perhaps every home in your community will have its own anaerobic digester power source or maybe your family's car will soon run on algae!

Aquaculture, the farming of water plants and animals for food, may be the future of first generation biomass energy. Algae are fast-growing plants that are full of oil. They are an excellent source of biodiesel. Think of this: 2.5 acres (1 ha) of land can produce 4,000 gallons (15,142 l) of corn-based ethanol, but 2.5 acres (1 ha) of algae can produce 26,000 ga (98,421 l) of oil! Algae grow quickly, so less space is needed. It would take only a space the size of Maine to grow enough algae to replace all the gasoline in the United States with algae-based biodiesel.

Algae is 50 percent oil and one of the fastest-growing plants on Earth.

Pros and Cons

Algae is not eaten on the same scale as corn or sugar cane, so using it as an energy crop does not threaten global food sources the way using corn and sugar cane might. Algae can be grown in salt water or wastewater, so it does not use up the freshwater supply and it will not be affected by **drought**. A drought is a long period of time during which there is very little or no rain.

Right now, growing algae and converting it into diesel is still expensive. Some experts say it will take another 25 years to make algae fuel affordable. However, there are some companies in the United States that sell fuels produced from algae. Governments around the world are paying for research to help make algae fuel cheaper to produce.

Drilling for oil and gas strips Earth of its resources. Algae farming is a much more sustainable way to generate energy from the sea.

The Energy Future: You Choose

The government of Brazil passed laws to encourage the development of ethanol because in the long run, it was cheaper and easier than using oil. In the 1970s, the cost of oil was high, so California started using biomass. In the 1980s, the price of oil dropped, making fossil fuels the cheaper choice for electricity production, so California stopped developing biomass. Some people argue that even though oil and coal are bad for the environment, they are necessary. Others say money must be spent to develop alternatives, because oil and coal are running out and they cause pollution and global climate change. What do you think? Should we pay more now? Why? What are the alternatives?

Power Up!

Biomass energy can be produced in ways that are good for the environment, or ways that may cause more damage. Our challenge is to ensure that biomass energy is produced in ways that protect the environment and global food sources. We need biomass energy to do a better job than the fossil fuels it replaces. The future of sustainable energy will be mixing together different options, depending on what works best in each community.

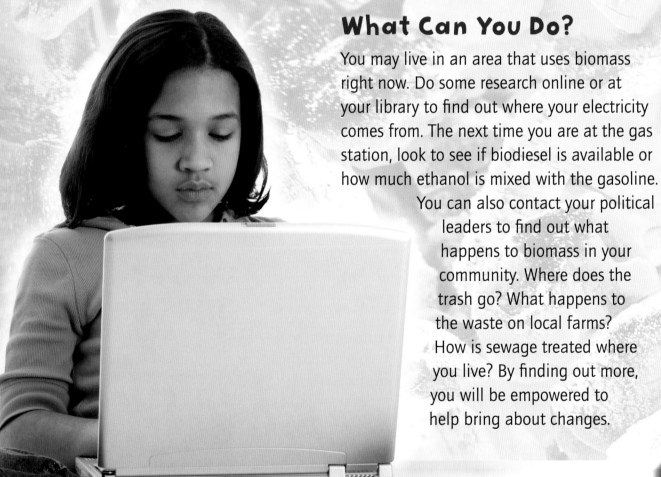

What Can You Do?

You may live in an area that uses biomass right now. Do some research online or at your library to find out where your electricity comes from. The next time you are at the gas station, look to see if biodiesel is available or how much ethanol is mixed with the gasoline. You can also contact your political leaders to find out what happens to biomass in your community. Where does the trash go? What happens to the waste on local farms? How is sewage treated where you live? By finding out more, you will be empowered to help bring about changes.

The more people know about biomass energy, the more likely they will use it in a sustainable way.

Activity

In anaerobic digestion, microorganisms break down organic material by eating it. We can turn the waste produced by these organisms into fuels such as alcohol or gas. Yeast is a microorganism that creates alcohol and carbon dioxide by eating sugar in a process called fermentation. In this activity, you will see yeast at work.

You Will Need:

- A teaspoon
- Yeast
- A small clear plastic bottle
- Warm water
- Sugar
- A party balloon

Instructions

1. Add 2 to 3 teaspoons (10–15 ml), or one packet, of yeast to the bottle.
2. Fill the bottle halfway with warm water, like the temperature of bath water. If the water is too hot, it will kill the yeast.
3. Add 4 to 6 tsp (20–30 ml) of sugar to the bottle.
4. Swirl the bottle to mix the water, sugar, and yeast together.
5. Put the opening of the balloon over the top of the bottle. Make sure the balloon seals the bottle opening.
6. Leave the bottle in a warm place, such as under a lamp, but away from open windows.
7. Check the bottle and balloon every 15 minutes to observe what happens.

What Happened?

Sugar is made of carbon and hydrogen. Water is made of hydrogen and oxygen. With sugar available, the heat allows the yeast organisms to remove the oxygen from the water and add carbon to make alcohol. Then it **expels**, or pushes out, the wastes. The extra oxygen is combined with carbon, making carbon dioxide. The balloon fills up as the carbon dioxide gas is produced and the sugary water starts turning into alcohol—you will be able to smell it when you take the balloon off the bottle. In the right amounts, this process produces ethanol fuel and returns carbon dioxide into the carbon cycle. What might happen if you changed the amount of sugar, water, or yeast? What if you used other sweet substances such as honey, corn syrup, or fruit juice? Try them and record your observations.

Glossary

Please note: Some bold-faced words are defined where they appear in the text

atmosphere The layer of gases that surround Earth

biochemical conversion Using microorganisms to turn biomass into a fuel

by-products The unintended materials created by a manufacturing process

carbohydrate An organic compound in food that is made up of complex sugar molecules

carbon cycle The continuous process in which carbon is exchanged between organisms and the environment

carbon dioxide A gas molecule made of a carbon atom joined with two oxygen atoms

chemical conversion Using chemical change to turn biomass into a fuel

civilization The most advanced stage of human social organization

climate change The increase in the temperature of the atmosphere near Earth's surface that can contribute to changes in global climate patterns

ethanol An alcohol that is used as fuel, and made by fermenting vegetation

fermentation A biochemical process in which yeast turns the sugars from plants into ethanol

fertilize To add substances to soil to make plants grow better

fossil fuels Energy sources made from the remains of plants and animals that died millions of years ago and were buried

gasification A chemical conversion process that turns solids into gases by heating them to high temperatures

greenhouse effect When atmospheric gases allow the Sun's energy to reach the surface, but prevent energy reflected off the surface from going back into space

Industrial Revolution A rapid change in which countries become more focused on using machines to make goods

microorganisms Organisms that can be seen only under a microscope

organic matter Material made up of organic compounds that contain carbon from plants and animals or their wastes

photosynthesis A process in which plants use sunlight to make food from carbon dioxide and water, creating carbon atoms that they use to grow, then releasing oxygen into the atmosphere

pollution Materials introduced into the environment and cause harmful or poisonous effects

power grid A network that takes electricity from power plants to consumers

renewable Describing something that renews itself once it is used

sewage A sludge containing human waste and other waste

sustainable Describing a way of living that conserves and efficiently uses natural resources

turbines Machines with rotating blades

Learning More

Find out more about biomass and alternative energy sources.

Books

Flounders, Anne. *Power for the Planet* (Our Green Earth). Red Chair Press, 2014.

Hand, Carol. *Biomass Energy* (Innovative Technologies). Abdo Group, 2013.

Owen, Ruth. *Energy from Plants and Trash: Biofuels and Biomass Power* (Power: Yesterday, Today, Tomorrow). PowerKids Press, 2013.

Spilsbury, Richard and Louise. *Biomass Power* (Let's Discuss Energy Resources). PowerKids Press, 2011.

Websites

Energy Kids is a website from the U.S. Energy Information Administration:
www.eia.gov/kids

Earth Day Canada's website has a lot of information and quizzes about energy at:
www.ecokids.ca

The Union of Concerned Scientists explains more about biomass energy at:
www.ucsusa.org/clean_energy/our-energy-choices/renewable-energy/ how-biomass-energy-works.html

Learn more about the science of biomass energy at:
http://epa.gov/climatestudents/solutions/technologies/biomass.html

Index